Contents

The Ref

They say he's blind,
They say he's deaf,
But he's in charge
Cos he's the Ref.

He makes defenders
Get their yards,
Gives diving forwards
Yellow cards.

He gives off-side,
Awards free kicks,
He red-cards cheats
For dirty tricks.

He spots the fouls
That fans do not,
Inside the box
Points to the spot.

He keeps the time,
He keeps the scores,
Cos he's the one
Who knows the laws.

Though no one ever
Knows his name,
The Ref's in charge
Of every game.

Rugby Players

You've a tear in your shorts and a hole
    in your shirt,
  A cut on your lip which you got in
    a scrum,
A tooth coming loose and a mouthful
    of dirt,
  A painful new bruise that's a pain in
    the bum,

You're covered in scratches and caked
    with dried blood,
  You're battered and splattered, there's
    soil in your hair,
You're slimy and grimy and covered
    in mud,
  But if you play rugby, you just do
    not care,

Cos rugby's a game for the tough and
    the rough,
  You like being messy, you like
    looking mean,
You're big and you're hard and you're
    made of strong stuff,
  And rugby's a game where you just
    can't stay clean.

There's only one thing that you don't
    like one bit –
And that's when it's your turn to wash
    the team kit!

On Your Marks, Get Set, Go!

You hit the track, a perfect start,
Your legs are pumping, so's your heart,

Your lungs are aching, fit to burst,
But you don't mind, you must come first,

You do your best, increase your speed,
You pass the rest, you're in the lead,

Just keep on going, round the bend,
Don't think of slowing till the end,

The final straight, increase the pace,
You cross the line – you've won the race!

Up for the Cup

The teams are picked,
The training's done,
The pre-match warm-ups
Have begun.

The pitch is marked,
The nets are up,
And every eye
Is on the cup.

There's goals and saves,
There's songs and cheers,
There's fans rejoicing,
Fans in tears.

There's headers, crosses,
Back-heel flicks,
There's penalties
And corner-kicks.

There's goal-kicks, throw-ins,
First-time balls,
Free kicks that bend
Around the walls.

There's dummies, shimmies,
Cheeky chips,
There's blatant dives
And clumsy trips.

There's clumsy tackles
That can hurt,
Defenders tugging
At your shirt.

There's sendings-off
And two-match bans,
There's yellow-cards
And stupid fans.

There's oohs and aahs
And shouts and roars,
The sound of 'Yes!'
When your team scores.

This game unites
The human race.
A football planet
Lost in space.

A world that keeps on
Spinning round,
A dream that never
Hits the ground.

The Defender

These forwards may be famous,
They may be very fast,
But I'm not impressed, cos I'm the best,
And no one's getting past.

With a CRUNCH! and a CRASH!
And a push in the back,
That's the end of another attack.

When I get the ball I hoof it,
Right up the other end,
If in doubt I put it out,
Cos my job's to defend.

With a CRUNCH! and a CRASH!
And a tug of the shirt,
A sliding tackle (I bet that hurt!)

Some people think I'm crazy,
They say that I can't play,
But you don't get beat, if you keep
                       a clean sheet
And I want it to stay that way.

With a CRUNCH! and a CRASH!
And he's flat on the floor,
I'm not going to let this forward score.

I don't care if they're skilful,
If they've got good close control,
I'll make them see that it's up to me
To keep them away from the goal.

With a CRUNCH! and a CRASH!
It wasn't that hard,
I don't believe it – I've got a red card!

The Fielder

I'm standing here at Deep Fine Leg,
With nothing much to do,
I've been stuck here since dinner-time,
(I'm bursting for the loo!)

This game is heading for a draw,
Of that there is no doubt,
Although there's only one man left
We just can't get him out.

It's hot out here, I'm feeling sleepy,
Hungry, tired and bored,
I wish that I was in the shade,
I wish that someone scored.

It's hard to see what's going on
The game's so far away,
It's sometimes hard to concentrate,
To keep up with the play.

Instead I watch a flock of birds
And count the passing clouds,
I wonder if I'm on TV,
And listen to the crowds.

One over left, and then we're off.
Six balls to win the match,
Just time to have a little snooze
And dream the perfect catch.

Hang on, what's this? Oh no! Oh dear,
The batsman's tried to score,
The ball is coming straight to me,
It's heading for a four!

I run and run and stretch and stretch,
I hear the crowds all shout,
I've dropped it – no – it's in my hand!
I've caught it – yes! He's out!

Training

Whatever your sport,
Whatever your game,
Everyone has to
Train the same.

No matter who you are,
It's no good complaining,
You won't be any good
Without any training.

You might be famous,
You might be rich,
But if you don't train
You'll get a stitch.

It may be hard,
It may be a pain,
But you won't be any good
If you don't train.

It might be hot,
It might be cold,
You might be young,
You might be old.

But if you don't put
The practice in,
You know in your heart
That you won't win.

The Batsman

One over left,
You're last man in;
You only need
Six runs to win.
You mark your crease
And dream of fame,
It's up to you
To win the game.
Six runs is all
You need to make,
Your heart beats fast,
Your fingers ache.

Your hands feel hot,
You're soaked in sweat,
Six runs is all
You need to get.
The bowler slowly
Walks uphill,
Then turns and runs
(You're feeling ill!)
The ball's released,
You watch it spin,
And tell yourself
'Six runs to win!'
The ball swings with
A wicked bounce,
The wicket keeper's
Set to pounce,
You go for six
And swing your bat,
You miss the ball –
Oh no! 'Owzat!'

Juan Pablo Montoya leads at the first bend.

Formula 1

The tension is mounting,
The crowds start to shout,
As on to the grid
The cars are pushed out.

The cars on the start-line
Rev-up to the max,
The crowd goes bananas
Alongside the tracks.

Then all of a sudden
There's no time to wait,
They take the first corner
And roar down the straight.

They hit the first bend
And squeeze through the gaps,
They fly round the track
For the next forty laps.

A pit-stop, a wheel-change,
Then back in the race,
There's just one lap left
As the drivers give chase.

But there's only one winner
And he's in the lead,
The checked-flag is his –
The champion of speed!

Football

Whistle, kick, pass, tackle,
Turn, pass, dribble, FLICK!

Whistle, kick, tackle, pass,
Turn, touch, dribble, KICK!

Whistle, kick, pass, tackle,
Turn, touch, dribble, BOOT!

Whistle, kick, tackle, pass,
Turn, touch, dribble, SHOOT!

Whistle, kick, pass, tackle,
Turn, touch, dribble, SHOUT!

Whistle, kick, tackle, pass,
Turn, touch, dribble, OUT!

Whistle, kick, pass, tackle,
Turn, touch, dribble, ROAR!

Whistle, kick, tackle, pass,
Turn, touch, dribble, S----!

Michael Owen scores!

The Striker

Defenders don't know what to do
When he is on the ball,
He twists and turns and shimmies through,
He curls it round the wall.

If he can get a shot at goal
They know that he's a threat,
With either foot or with his head
He'll bang it in the net.

He never misses penalties,
He's good at one-on-one,
And if you try man-marking him
One turn and he is gone.

If he escapes the off-side trap
Defenders get upset,
Because they know that if he shoots
He'll bang it in the net.

He dribbles past the full-backs,
He's even megged a sweeper,
He out-jumps them at corners
To head it past the keeper.

The fans all love the striker
Who won't let them forget,
That if you give him half a chance
He'll bang it in the net.

There's Nothing to Do

'There's nothing to do,' said Fred,
   'it's doing in my head.'
'Let's play tennis,' said Dennis.

'There's nothing to do,' said Fred,
   'it's doing in my head.'
'Let's play lacrosse,' said Ross.

'There's nothing to do,' said Fred,
   'it's doing in my head.'
'Let's play squash,' said Josh.

'There's nothing to do,' said Fred,
   'it's doing in my head.'
'Let's go for a swim,' said Kim.

'There's nothing to do,' said Fred,
   'it's doing in my head.'
'Let's go for a ride on a pony,' said Tony.

'There's nothing to do,' said Fred,
   'it's doing in my head.'
'Let's go for a dive,' said Clive.

'There's nothing to do,' said Fred,
   'it's doing in my head.'
'Let's play golf,' said Rolf.

'There's nothing to do,' said Fred,
   'it's doing in my head.'
'Let's go for ride on a bike,' said Mike.

'There's nothing to do,' said Fred,
    'it's doing in my head.'
'Let's play basketball,' said Paul.

'There's nothing to do,' said Fred,
    'it's doing in my head.'
'Let's pole-vault,' said Walt.

'There's nothing to do,' said Fred,
    'it's doing in my head.'
'Let's roller-blade,' said Jade.

'There's nothing to do,' said Fred,
    'it's doing in my head.'
'Let's go to the gym,' said Tim.

'There's too much to do,' said Fred,
    'it's doing in my head,
I know what I'll do – I'm going to bed.'